~FOUR~
Sides the Same

A Book About Squares

by Christianne C. Jones   illustrated by Ronnie Rooney

Special thanks to our advisers for their expertise:
Stuart Farm, M.Ed., Mathematics Lecturer
University of North Dakota

Susan Kesselring, M.A., Literacy Educator
Rosemount-Apple Valley-Eagan (Minnesota) School District

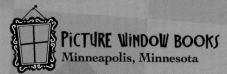
PICTURE WINDOW BOOKS
Minneapolis, Minnesota

Editor: Jill Kalz

Designer: Joe Anderson

Creative Director: Keith Griffin

Editorial Director: Carol Jones

The illustrations in this book were created in acrylic paints.

Picture Window Books

5115 Excelsior Boulevard

Suite 232

Minneapolis, MN 55416

877-845-8392

www.picturewindowbooks.com

Printed in the United States of America.

Library of Congress Cataloging-in-Publication Data

Jones, Christianne C.

Four sides the same : a book about squares / by Christianne C. Jones ; illustrated by

Ronnie Rooney.

p. cm. – (Know your shapes)

Includes bibliographical references and index.

ISBN 1-4048-1574-0

1. Square–Juvenile literature. I. Rooney, Ronnie, ill. II. Title.

QA482.J66 2006

516'.154–dc22

2005021844

Shapes are all around. You can find them everywhere you look. Shapes can be tall and skinny, short and round, long and wide. Some shapes will look the same, and some will look different, but they are all amazing. Let's find some shapes!

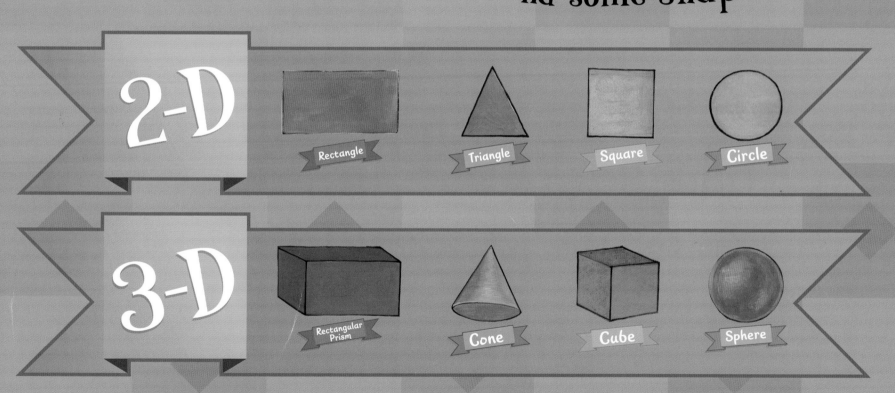

2-D
Rectangle
Triangle
Square
Circle

3-D
Rectangular Prism
Cone
Cube
Sphere

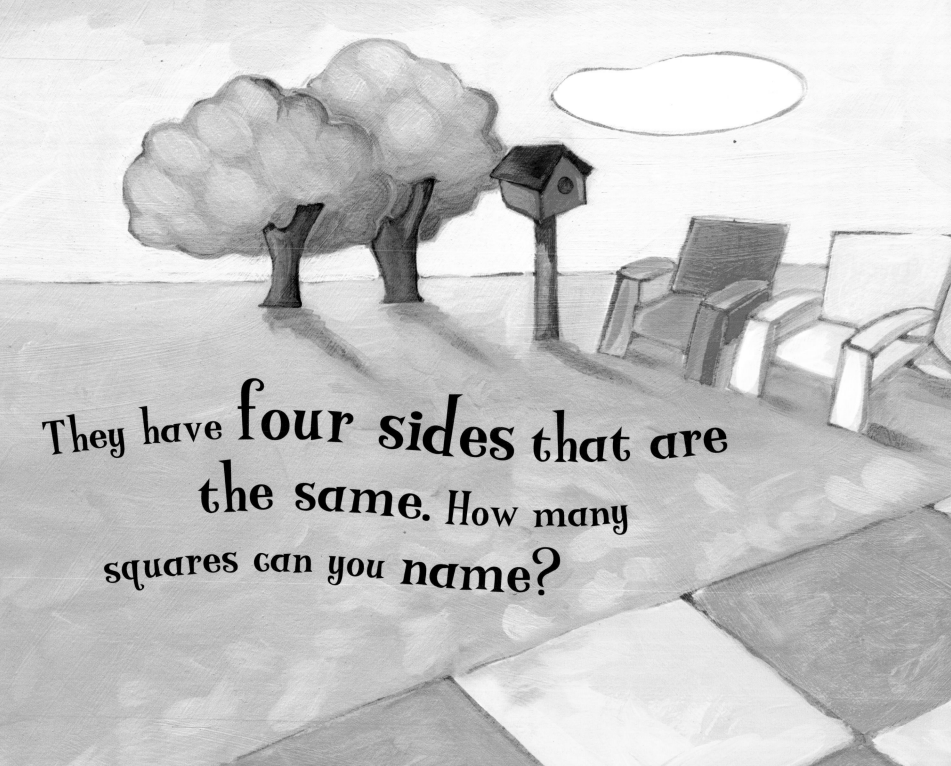

They have **four sides** that are the same. How many squares can you **name**?

A yellow square tells me what to do.

Come to the backyard

HOME SWEET HOME

A **glass square** is easy to see through.

A **soft square** covers the grass.

Tasty squares disappear fast!

13

14

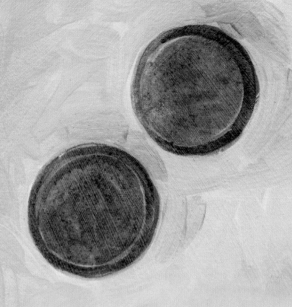

A checkered square
is fun to play.

Colorful squares
start to sway.

A **sandy square** tickles our fingers and toes.

A soapy square cleans all of our clothes.

Squares are everywhere, if you look. You already found a lot inside this book!

MEMORY SQUARES

WHAT YOU NEED:
- Four sheets of construction paper (all one color)
- Scissors
- Crayons or markers
- A friend

WHAT YOU DO:
1. Have an adult cut each sheet in half across the middle. Then cut those two pieces in half. Each sheet should make four cards.
2. Draw a picture of something square on the back of one card. Draw the same picture on the back of another card.
3. Repeat step 2 until you have eight different pairs.
4. Shuffle the cards and lay them face down.
5. Have your friend flip over two cards. If they match, he or she gets to go again. If they don't match, flip the cards back over. Now, it's your turn. The player who finds the most pairs wins!

TO LEARN MORE

AT THE LIBRARY

Bruce, Lisa. *Patterns in the Park*. Chicago: Raintree, 2004.

Burke, Jennifer S. *Squares*. New York: Children's Press, 2000.

Schuette, Sarah L. *Squares*. Mankato, Minn.: A+ Books, 2003.

Scott, Janine. *The Shapes of Things*. Minneapolis: Compass Point Books, 2003.

ON THE WEB

FactHound offers a safe, fun way to find Internet sites related to this book. All of the sites on FactHound have been researched by our staff.
1. Visit *www.facthound.com*
2. Type in this special code for age-appropriate sites: 1404815740
3. Click on the FETCH IT button.

Your trusty FactHound will fetch the best sites for you!

FUN FACTS

- Two-dimensional (2-D) shapes are flat. They have just a front and a back. Three-dimensional (3-D) shapes have a front, a back, and sides. A cube is a 3-D square.

- The game of checkers is more than 5,000 years old. People first played it around 3000 B.C.

- The first washing machine designed for home use was made in 1874. William Blackstone built it as a gift for his wife's birthday.

LOOK FOR ALL OF THE BOOKS IN THE KNOW YOUR SHAPES SERIES:

Around the Park: A Book About Circles 1-4048-1572-4

Four Sides the Same: A Book About Squares 1-4048-1574-0

Party of Three: A Book About Triangles 1-4048-1575-9

Two Short, Two Long: A Book About Rectangles 1-4048-1573-2